THE BEST OF

1997

'Hi, honey, I'm cloned'

MATTHEW PRITCHETT studied at St Martin's School of Art in London and first saw himself published in the *New Statesman* during one of its rare lapses from high seriousness. He has been *The Daily Telegraph*'s front-page pocket cartoonist since 1988. In 1995 he was the winner of the Cartoon Arts Trust Award and was Cartoonist of the Year in 1992 and 1996.

D1328891

The Daily Telegraph

THE BEST OF

1997

ORION

Orion Books
A Division of the Orion Publishing Group Ltd
Orion House
5 Upper St Martin's Lane
London WC2H 9EA

First published by Orion in 1997

A CIP catalogue record for this book is available
from the British Library

ISBN 0 75280 917 2

Printed and bound in Great Britain by
The Guernsey Press Co. Ltd, Guernsey, Channel Islands

THE BEST OF

'Jenkins, it looks like you'll be getting my dinner in your free time from now on'

Sporting Matters

Estonia stand up the Scots at international

'Are you Frankie Dettori? Can I have your autograph?'

Jockey wins seven in a row

Sporting Matters

The Hello File

'Apparently, some members
of Oasis have difficulty
in mating if there's too
much media attention'

Liam and Patsy's on-off wedding

RICHARD
BRANSON
BALLOONS

Branson's latest record
attempt fails

The Hello File

'It's the latest Conran table'

Terence Conran gets a divorce

Uptown, Down Home

'Typical, here come the urban foxes, down for the weekend'

'I'm going to eat you, but I assure you it has nothing to do with class envy'

Religious Affairs

'I've been thinking of running away with a divorcee . . . hello . . . is anyone there?'

Catholic priest disappears with lover

'My dad is higher up in the Catholic church than your dad'

'Fathers' and fatherhood

Religious Affairs

'Fortunately, our Catholic priest doesn't seem too interested in Labour's child benefit reforms'

'I do consider myself a Labour voter, although I don't actually go to the polling station'

The Church comes out for Labour

European Unions

French roadblocks trap
UK drivers

'Monetary Union? Well...er,
it's when two currencies who
love each other...er...join
together...um. Look, can't
we talk about this when
you're older?'

Not in front of the children

European Unions

'It's worse than I thought – I'm going to have to renegotiate Britain's whole position in the EU'

Social chapter threatens industrial investment

The Prison Service

'Come in number 45823929,
your time is up'

The Prison Service

Automatic right to jury trial in question
as some prisoners released in error

The Prison Service

'Oh, er....STOP THE BYPASS!'

'I'm coaxing it back to the open sea'

Two topical ways to escape...

Defensive Manoeuvres

Defensive Manoeuvres

'Somewhere out there there's a war pension without my name on it'

Government attacked over missing pensions and Gulf pesticides

Service as Normal

'Good news, the Health Secretary says you'll have your operation before Britain joins a single currency'

'He threw himself downstairs just so he could meet women'

Service as Normal

'I've never helped a patient to die, but I sometimes think my receptionist might have'

Service as Normal

'Scalpel, swab, apple sauce...'

'Right, I'm just going to pop behind the screen and change into a woman'

Transsexual doctor reveals all

Time for a Change

'I feel uneasy – nothing dreadful has happened for 20 minutes'

And they're off...

Time for a Change

'Would you like our manifesto any better if it tasted of chocolate?'

Child-friendly vegetables launched

'My husband's got out his election soap box'

Time for a Change

'And we plan to pay for all our spending commitments with a windfall tax on the Duchess of York'

'Our plan is for your lifeless body to be washed up on a beach carrying our fake election strategy...'

Things start to get dirty...

Time for a Change

Tories split up as Labour are shut up

Time for a Change

'Well, we've certainly licked the complacency problem'

Labour accused of complacency –
not a problem for the Tories...

Time for a Change

Hamilton v Bell: it's war in the shires

Time for a Change

'This is Bosnia TV reporting from strife-torn Tatton'

'All I'm saying is, I bet Mrs Hamilton laughs at her husband's dinner party jokes'

Time for a Change

'Now?'

'Will you read me the story about the tortoise and the hare just one more time?'

Polls continue to show huge Labour lead

Time for a Change

'I'm going on one last frantic whistle-stop tour of the kitchen – do you want a cup of cocoa?'

Events reach fever pitch

'You're wearing the same shirt you wear every Thursday, you're eating the same breakfast, sitting in the same chair, you're catching the same train to work as you always do, and now you're trying to tell me you're voting for change!'

Time for a Change

'A case of your least smug champagne, please'

Labour quietly confident

'Come on, move along now, there's nothing to see'

As the Tories go messily

Now They're In

'It's amazing to think
he's only ever known
a Labour government'

'We want a honeymoon just
like the Labour Party's'

The first days of the new government

Now They're In

'Hello, gorgeous, come on,
give us a smile...'

Blair's children move into Downing St.
as 'Blair's Babes' move into Westminster

Now They're In

'I do like you, Alan, but just as a friend, not in a Blair, Clinton kind of way'

GALLUP: BLAIR MOST POPULAR PM EVER

'Daddy, why does Tony Blair allow earthquakes to happen?'

Blair enjoys halcyon beginning at home and abroad

Now They're In

'The Devolution White Paper is all right as long as you don't think about what's in it'

'Darling, am I in favour of self rule?'

The big question...

And Meanwhile

The Tories fight over the remains of their party

And Meanwhile

'Among the leadership contenders are: Baby Tory, Scary Tory, Posh Tory, Sporty Tory and Ginger Tory...'

Spicing up the leadership race

'I married you because you were the least worst option'

The Anti-Clarke vote wins out

Alcopops With Rosie

Alcopops With Rosie

'Give me an ice lolly – you'd better make that a double'

'Remind me, is it Thickhead or Two Dogs that one drinks with fish?'

Government Health Warning

'I gave up smoking after I was shown an X-ray of my wallet'

Bad news for smokers

'We've put nicotine patches over the names of the tobacco companies'

Government Health Warning

'I'm going to quit smoking –
I'm worried I'll get skin
cancer standing out here'

'Could you hide those
cigarettes inside a copy
of Gay News?'

Good news for gays as age
of consent is lowered

Weather Warning

'Have you met my husband?
He's a weather forecaster'

'Apparently, this is the wettest
drought since records began'

Weathermen predict wet May and drought
in June – with their usual accuracy

Weather Warning

'Wow, fantastic, man!
Pass this round'

Weather Warning

Weather Warning

And after that a
winter of extremes

Warning Tone

'It's time to take the telephone out of Irish politics'

IRA hoaxes cause motorway chaos

As Sinn Fein carry on regardless

The Swampy Factor

'Some people find bypass protesters unpleasant, but they're very good for the soil'

'SWAMPY!'

Silly Season

'When Daddy Blair got home he said "who's been playing with my Millennium Dome?"'

The Millennium Dome project runs into
trouble while Blair is on holiday

Silly Season

'How ironic, we've just had a near miss with the plane my luggage is on'

'Isn't that the nice couple we had a near miss with last year?'

Two near miss stories come dangerously close together

Silly Season

'I think the surgeon's 16-year-old daughter helped with the operation'

'And that grey area there is your bed, which is what we'll be removing'

Surgeon's daughter does her bit to reduce growing waiting lists

Now You See It, Now You Don't

'Call a Channel 5 re-tuner,
everything is swirling
around and blurred'

'Forget about Hale-Bopp,
I've just caught a
glimpse of Channel 5'

Extra terrestrial tv channel is launched

It's a Mad, Mad, Mad, World

BSE continues to be a feature

It's a Mad, Mad, Mad, World

Cloning

'You're two in a million, baby'

'Eureka! I've cloned mint sauce'

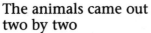

The animals came out
two by two

Space 1997

'It's one small dent for Mir,
a giant leap for our
insurance premium'

Russian space station in trouble

GARAGE

'If this car was a space-station
I'd tell you to get into the
emergency module and
return to Earth'

Space 1997

While Rover looks
for life on Mars…

Law & Order

'We don't let him watch the
Home Secretary on TV – it
encourages him to act tough'

Government gets
tough on crime

'Michael Howard wants to
have a word with you about
the state of my bedroom'

And on the parents
of juvenile criminals

Law & Order

'I wanted to buy a potato peeling knife but I had some problem with the definition'

Knife ban proves difficult

'Did you teach him to beg? Next he'll be involved in graffiti and petty crime'

Zero tolerance reaches UK

Law & Order

'And how long has this lamb been stalking you, Mary?'

'Our speed camera has run out of film so I've done this artist's impression of you'

Money, Money, Money

'This won't change my way of life – I'll still show up for work and see my old mates'

'If you want a cat of my calibre, you have to feed me the going rate'

The fat cats are still with us...

Educating the Nation

'I'm afraid your car failed the tough new emissions test, but it did get six GCSEs'

Problem schools named as exam results questioned

Educating the Nation

'Ah, I'd recognise an old
Ridings school tie anywhere'

Hit squads go into
Yorkshire problem school

'I can't help thinking that if I
had been caned at school none
of this would have happened'

Carry On British Airways

'And Damien Hirst did the tail fin on this one'

'I hate airports – I'm terrified of not flying'

BA replace union flag with tailfin artworks as cabin crew decide to strike

Carry On British Airways

'Oh brilliant! The day we can get 10 francs to the pound is the same damned day we can't get to France'

'I've got a sick note for a migraine, could you upgrade me to bronchitis?'

Those not on strike go off sick

Life – It'll Cost You

'Could you knock a bit off the tuition fees as I don't intend to go to many lectures?'

'I note that your essay is overdue. You have been charged £25 for this letter'

Government plans to charge for university tuition

Life – It'll Cost You

'I'm £10,000 in debt after being at the university of life'

And roads…

Life – It'll Cost You

'Your bank manager says
just take two aspirin'

And health…

'I thought MIRAS was a
quarter-finalist at Wimbledon'

And mortgages…

Miscellaneous

'Hey, a special stamp to commemorate the post strikes'

'At the third stroke your new telephone code will be ...'

Telephone area codes change again...

Miscellaneous

'Man has been standing upright for six million years and now he'd like to sit down for forty minutes'

'My grandparents are at that worrying age when they're out all night at Rolling Stones concerts'

Scientists discover that modern man has been around even longer than the Rolling Stones

Miscellaneous

'Don't drive to work, follow
Tony Blair's example and
charter Concorde'

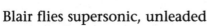

Blair flies supersonic, unleaded

'He's feeding well but I'm
worried that he still hasn't
done anything about
his pension'

Miscellaneous

Walker reveals she didn't...

'How was it for you?'

'Get a job? And risk
overheating the economy?
No thank you!'

'I'm knitting a job application'

Welfare to work...

Miscellaneous

'I know I agreed to be a surrogate mother, but I've decided I want to keep 20,000 of them'

'I want to go privately'

Miscellaneous

'Usually we go to the River Oder for our summer holiday, but this year we're going all over eastern Germany'

'This isn't the first time you've been up before me, is it?'

Miscellaneous

'LOOK! I'M PAYING MY
HOTEL BILL MYSELF WITH
MY OWN MONEY!'

'I picked up these brown
envelopes here last week and
there was nothing inside them'

Miscellaneous

'I fell off the
moral high ground'

Mr Swann, I'm afraid that
'overall I'm better off' is not
good enough for tax purposes

Miscellaneous